THE PICT
DORIAN

Can a painting of a person tell you more about him than the person's own face? If it is painted with love, perhaps the painting will show more than just the outside of that person – perhaps it will show the inside.

We often say that a face is like an open book: 'the face tells its own story,' we say. When Dorian Gray sees the painting of his own face, he falls in love with his own beauty. Nothing must touch his beauty, nothing must hurt or change it – not love, not even time. And so he cuts the link between his face and his heart, between his outside and his inside. His face does not change; it stays young and beautiful. But the picture – painted with love – tells the true story. It shows the real Dorian Gray, who is growing old and ugly and full of hate.

OXFORD BOOKWORMS LIBRARY
Fantasy & Horror

The Picture of Dorian Gray

Stage 3 (1000 headwords)

Series Editor: Jennifer Bassett
Founder Editor: Tricia Hedge
Activities Editors: Jennifer Bassett and Alison Baxter

OSCAR WILDE

The Picture of Dorian Gray

Retold by
Jill Nevile

OXFORD UNIVERSITY PRESS

OXFORD
UNIVERSITY PRESS

Great Clarendon Street, Oxford OX2 6DP

Oxford University Press is a department of the University of Oxford.
It furthers the University's objective of excellence in research, scholarship,
and education by publishing worldwide in

Oxford New York

Auckland Cape Town Dar es Salaam Hong Kong Karachi
Kuala Lumpur Madrid Melbourne Mexico City Nairobi
New Delhi Shanghai Taipei Toronto

With offices in

Argentina Austria Brazil Chile Czech Republic France Greece
Guatemala Hungary Italy Japan Poland Portugal Singapore
South Korea Switzerland Thailand Turkey Ukraine Vietnam

OXFORD and OXFORD ENGLISH are registered trade marks of
Oxford University Press in the UK and in certain other countries

This simplified edition © Oxford University Press 2008

Database right Oxford University Press (maker)

First published in Oxford Bookworms 1989

16 18 20 19 17 15

ISBN 978 0 19 479126 7

A complete recording of this Bookworms edition of
The Picture of Dorian Gray is available on audio CD ISBN 978 0 19 479098 7

Printed in China

ACKNOWLEDGEMENTS
Illustrated by: Nick Harris

CONTENTS

The Artist

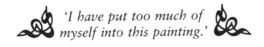 *'I have put too much of myself into this painting.'*

1

Through the open windows of the room came the rich scent of summer flowers. Lord Henry Wotton lay back in his chair and smoked his cigarette. Beyond the soft sounds of the garden he could just hear the noise of London.

In the centre of the room there was a portrait of a very beautiful young man, and in front of it stood the artist himself, Basil Hallward.

'It's your best work, Basil, the best portrait that you've ever painted,' said Lord Henry lazily. 'You must send it to the best art gallery in London.'

'No,' Basil said slowly. 'No, I won't send it anywhere.'

Lord Henry was surprised. 'But my dear Basil, why not?' he asked. 'What strange people you artists are! You want to be famous, but then you're not happy when you *are* famous. It's bad when people talk about you – but it's much worse when they *don't* talk about you.'

'I know you'll laugh at me,' replied Basil, 'but I can't exhibit the picture in an art gallery. I've put too much of myself into it.'

Lord Henry laughed. 'Too much of yourself into it! You don't look like him at all. He has a fair and beautiful face. And you – well, you look intelligent, of course, but with

'It's the best portrait that you've ever painted,'
said Lord Henry.

your strong face and black hair, you are not beautiful.'

'You don't understand me, Harry,' replied Basil. (Lord Henry's friends always called him Harry.) 'Of course I'm not like him,' Basil continued. 'In fact, I prefer not to be beautiful. Dorian Gray's beautiful face will perhaps bring him danger and trouble.'

'Dorian Gray? Is that his name?' asked Lord Henry.

'Yes. But I didn't want to tell you.'

'Why not?'

'Oh, I can't explain,' said Basil. 'When I like people a lot, I never tell their names to my other friends. I love secrets, that's all.'

'Of course,' agreed his friend. 'Life is much more exciting when you have secrets. For example, I never know where my wife is, and my wife never knows what I'm doing. When we meet – and we do meet sometimes – we tell each other crazy stories, and we pretend that they're true.'

'You pretend all the time, Harry,' said Basil. 'I think that you're probably a very good husband, but you like to hide your true feelings.'

'Oh, don't be so serious, Basil,' smiled Lord Henry. 'Let's go into the garden.'

2

In the garden the leaves shone in the sunlight, and the flowers moved gently in the summer wind. The two young men sat on a long seat under the shadow of a tall tree.

'Before I go,' said Lord Henry, 'you must answer my question, Basil. Why won't you exhibit Dorian Gray's portrait in an art gallery?' He looked at his friend and smiled. 'Please give me the *real* reason, now. Not the answer that you gave me before.'

'Harry, when an artist feels strongly about a portrait, it becomes a portrait of himself, not of the sitter. The artist paints the face and body of the sitter, but in fact he shows his own feelings. The reason why I won't exhibit this portrait is because I'm afraid it shows the secret of my heart.'

Lord Henry laughed. 'And what *is* this secret of your heart?'

His friend was silent. Lord Henry picked a flower and looked at it with interest.

'Two months ago,' Basil said at last, 'I was at a party at Lady Brandon's house. I was talking to friends when I realized that someone was watching me. I turned and saw Dorian Gray for the first time. We looked at each other, and I felt a sudden, very strong fear. I felt that this person could change my life . . . could bring me happiness – and unhappiness. Later, Lady Brandon introduced us. We laughed at something that she said, and became friends at once.'

He stopped. Lord Henry smiled. 'Tell me more,' he said. 'How often do you see him?'

'Every day,' answered Basil. 'I'm not happy if I don't see him every day – he's necessary to my life.'

'But I thought you only cared about your art,' said Lord Henry.

'He *is* all my art now,' replied Basil, seriously. 'Since I met Dorian Gray, the work that I've done is good, the best work

'I'm afraid that the picture shows the secret of
my heart,' said Basil.

of my life. Because of him I see art in a different way, a new way. When I'm with him, I paint wonderful pictures.'

'Basil, this is extraordinary. I must meet Dorian Gray,' said Lord Henry.

Basil got up and walked up and down the garden. 'So that's my secret. Dorian doesn't know about my feelings. And I can't let people see the portrait, because it shows what's in my heart. There's too much of myself in it, Harry, too much!'

Lord Henry looked at Basil's face before he spoke. 'Tell me, does Dorian Gray care about you?'

The artist thought for a few moments. 'He likes me,' he said at last. 'I know he likes me. Usually he's very friendly to me, but sometimes he seems to enjoy hurting me. He says unkind things that give me pain, Harry. And then I feel that I've given myself to somebody who thinks my heart is a pretty flower. A flower that he can enjoy for a summer's day, and can forget tomorrow.'

'Summer days, Basil,' said Lord Henry with a smile, 'can sometimes be too long. Perhaps you'll become tired sooner than he will.'

'Harry, don't talk like that. While I live, Dorian Gray will be important to me. You change your feelings too quickly. You can't feel what I feel.'

'My dear Basil, how unkind you are!' Lord Henry was amused. How interesting other people's lives were, he thought. Slowly he pulled a flower to pieces with his long fingers. 'I remember now,' he continued. 'I think my aunt knows Dorian Gray. I'd like to meet him very much.'

'But I don't want you to meet him,' said Basil.

A servant came across the garden towards them.

'Mr Dorian Gray has arrived, sir,' he said to Basil.

'You have to introduce me now,' laughed Lord Henry.

Basil turned to him. 'Dorian Gray is my dearest friend,' he said quietly. 'He's a good person and he's young – only twenty. Don't change him. Don't try to influence him. Your clever words are very amusing, of course, but you laugh at serious things. Don't take him away from me. He's necessary to my life as an artist.'

Lord Henry smiled. 'You worry too much, my friend,' he said, and together they walked back into the house.

The Friend

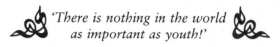

3

As they entered the house, they saw Dorian Gray. He was sitting by the window and turning some pages of music.

'You must lend me this music, Basil,' he said. Then he turned and saw Lord Henry. 'Oh, I'm sorry, Basil. I didn't realize . . .'

'Dorian, this is Lord Henry Wotton,' said Basil. 'He's an old friend of mine.'

Dorian Gray shook hands with Lord Henry, and while they talked, Lord Henry studied the young man. Yes, he was very good-looking indeed, with his bright blue eyes and his gold hair. He had an open, honest face. There were no dark secrets in that face. Lord Henry could understand Basil's feelings for him.

Basil was getting his paints ready. Now he looked at Lord Henry. 'Harry,' he said, 'I want to finish this portrait of Dorian today. I'm afraid I must ask you to go away.'

Lord Henry smiled and looked at Dorian Gray. 'Should I go, Mr Gray?' he asked.

'Oh, please don't leave, Lord Henry. Basil never talks when he's painting, and it's so boring. Please stay. I'd like you to talk to me.'

'Well, Basil?' Lord Henry asked.

The artist bit his lip. 'Very well, Harry. Stay . . . if you must.'

While Basil painted, Lord Henry talked, and the young man listened. The words filled Dorian's head like music – wild, exciting music. What a beautiful voice Lord Henry has, he thought. They are only words, but how terrible they are! How bright and dangerous! You cannot escape from words. Dorian began to understand things about himself that he had never understood before. Why had he never seen himself so clearly, he wondered?

Lord Henry watched Dorian, and smiled. He knew when to speak, and when to be silent. He felt very interested in this young man, with his wonderful face.

Later they walked in the garden together, while Basil worked at the portrait. The rich scent of the flowers was all around them. Dorian looked at the older man, and wondered about him. He was tall, with a thin dark face and cool white hands. Dorian liked him, but why did he feel a little afraid of him?

'You must come out of the sun, Mr Gray,' said Lord Henry. 'A brown skin isn't fashionable and it won't suit you.'

'Oh, it doesn't matter,' laughed Dorian.

'But it *should* matter to you, Mr Gray.'

'Why?' asked Dorian.

'Because you're young, and being young is wonderful. Ah, you smile. You don't think so now, but one day you'll understand what I mean – when you're old, and tired, and no longer beautiful. You have a wonderfully beautiful face, Mr Gray. It's true. Don't shake your head at me. And there's nothing more important, more valuable than beauty. When

'When your youth goes, your beauty will go with it,'
said Lord Henry.

your youth goes, your beauty will go with it. Then you'll suddenly discover that your life is empty – there will be nothing to enjoy, nothing to hope for. Time is your enemy, Mr Gray. It will steal everything from you. People are afraid of themselves today. Afraid to live. But you, with your face and your youth, there's nothing that you cannot do. You must live! Live the wonderful life that is in you! We can never be young again. Youth! Ah, there is nothing in the world as important as youth!'

Dorian Gray listened and wondered. New ideas filled his head. He felt strange, different.

At that moment Basil called them from the house. Lord Henry turned to Dorian. 'You're happy that you've met me, Mr Gray,' he said.

'Yes, I'm happy now. Will I always be happy, I wonder?'

'Always!' Lord Henry smiled. 'What a terrible word! Women use it much too often. What does it mean? It's today that is important.'

4

In the house Basil Hallward stood in front of the portrait of Dorian Gray. 'It's finished,' he said. He wrote his name in the corner of the picture.

Lord Henry studied the picture carefully. 'Yes,' he said. 'It's your best work. It's excellent. Mr Gray, come and look at yourself.'

Dorian looked at the picture for a long time. He smiled as he saw the beautiful face in front of him, and for a moment he felt happy. But then he remembered Lord Henry's words. 'How long', he thought, 'will I look like the picture? Time will steal my beauty from me. I will grow old, but the picture will always be young.' And his heart grew cold with fear.

'Don't you like it, Dorian?' asked Basil at last.

'Of course he likes it,' said Lord Henry. 'It's a very fine work of art. I'd like to buy it myself.'

'It's not mine to sell, Harry. The picture is Dorian's.'

'I wish,' cried Dorian suddenly, 'I wish that I could always stay young and that the picture could grow old.'

Lord Henry laughed. 'I don't think you would like that, Basil, would you?'

'No, I wouldn't like it at all,' agreed Basil with a smile.

Dorian turned, his face red and angry. 'Yes, you like your art better than your friends,' he said to Basil. 'How long will you like me? Only while I'm beautiful, I suppose. Lord Henry is right. Youth is the most important thing in the world. Oh, why did you paint this picture? Why should it stay young while I grow old? I wish the picture could change, and I could stay as I am. I would give anything, yes, anything, for that.' He hid his face in his hands.

'Dorian, Dorian!' said Basil unhappily. 'Don't talk like that. You're my dearest friend.' He turned to Lord Henry. 'What have you been teaching him?' he asked angrily. 'Why didn't you go away when I asked you?'

Lord Henry smiled. 'It's the real Dorian Gray – that's all.'

Basil turned and walked quickly over to the portrait. 'It's my best work, but now I hate it. I will destroy it now, before it destroys our friendship.' He picked up a long knife.

'I wish that I could always stay young and that the picture
could grow old,' cried Dorian.

But Dorian was there before him. 'No, Basil, don't! You can't destroy it. That would be murder!'

'So,' said Basil coldly, 'you've decided that you like the portrait after all.'

'Like it?' said Dorian. 'I'm in love with it. I cannot live without it.'

Later, during tea, Lord Henry invited Basil and Dorian to go with him to the theatre that night. Basil refused, but Dorian was happy to accept.

'Stay and have dinner with me, Dorian,' said Basil, but no, Dorian preferred to go to the theatre with Lord Henry.

As the door closed behind Dorian and Lord Henry, Basil turned back to the picture. 'I shall stay here with the real Dorian Gray,' he said sadly to himself.

5

The next morning Lord Henry went to visit his aunt, Lady Agatha. She was surprised to see him.

'I thought you fashionable young men never got up until the afternoon,' she said.

'Ah, but my dear aunt, I need some information, you see,' replied Lord Henry. 'I met Dorian Gray yesterday, and I'd like to know more about him.'

'Oh, he's Lord Kelso's grandson,' said Lady Agatha. 'His mother was Lady Margaret Devereux, a very beautiful woman. She ran away from home to marry a poor soldier. He was killed a few months later and she died soon after her son was born. She was a lovely woman. Dorian Gray has her beauty and he will, I understand, have his grandfather's money.'

'He is', agreed Lord Henry, 'extraordinarily good-looking.'

'Come to lunch,' invited his aunt. 'Dorian Gray will be here and you can meet him again.'

'I'd love to come,' smiled Lord Henry.

As he left, Lord Henry thought about this sad story. He became more interested than ever in this beautiful young man, Dorian Gray. He remembered the night before, when Dorian had watched him with his bright blue eyes, half wondering, half afraid. 'He does not yet know himself,' thought Lord Henry, with a smile. 'But I can teach him. Yes, I can influence him in any way that I please. I will teach him to discover the fire of youth, and love, and life.'

The conversation among the fashionable people at Lady Agatha's lunch was quick and clever. Lord Henry talked, in his lazy, amusing way, and knew that Dorian Gray was watching and listening.

After a while the conversation turned to a friend's plans to marry an American girl.

'Why can't these American women stay in their own country? They're always telling us that it's a paradise for women,' said Lord Burdon.

'It is,' said Lord Henry. 'That's the reason why they're so happy to escape from it.'

'They say,' laughed the man next to Lady Agatha, 'that when good Americans die, they go to Paris.'

'Really! And where do bad Americans go to when they die?' asked Lady Agatha.

Dorian Gray never took his eyes away from Lord Henry.

'They go to America,' said Lord Henry.

People smiled, and the conversation moved on to other things. Lord Henry took ideas and played with them; he gave them wings, and they flew like brightly coloured birds around the room. People laughed, and smiled, and told him that he should be more serious. But Dorian Gray never took his eyes away from Lord Henry.

After lunch Lord Henry said that he was going to the park and as he left the room, Dorian Gray touched his arm. 'May I come with you?' he asked.

'But I thought you'd promised to go and see Basil Hallward,' Lord Henry replied.

'Yes, but I'd prefer to come with you. Please let me,' said Dorian. 'I want to listen to you talking. Nobody speaks as well as you do.'

'Ah! I've talked enough for today.' Lord Henry smiled. 'But you may come with me if you want to.'

The Young Man in Love

 'Love is a more wonderful thing than art.'

6

One afternoon, a month later, Dorian Gray visited Lord Henry. Dorian was excited and his eyes were shining.

'Harry,' he began, 'I'm discovering life. I'm doing everything that you told me to do. I'm in love!'

'Who are you in love with?' asked Lord Henry, calmly.

'With an actress.'

'Oh, everybody's in love with an actress at some time in their lives,' said Lord Henry.

'No, Harry, this is different. She's wonderful! Her name's Sybil Vane, and one day she'll be a very famous actress. She really is extraordinarily clever.'

'My dear boy,' said Lord Henry in his lazy voice, 'no woman is extraordinarily clever. Women have nothing to say, but they say it beautifully. There are only five women in London who can give you real conversation. But tell me about your wonderful actress. How long have you known her?'

'Harry! I'll tell you all about her, but you must promise not to laugh.'

Lord Henry listened and smiled. Dorian had discovered an old, dirty theatre in a poor street in London. He had gone in to look for adventure, but had found love, he told Lord

'*I went in to look for adventure, but I found love,*'
Dorian told Lord Henry.

Henry. The play had been Shakespeare's *Romeo and Juliet*.

'Romeo was a fat old man with a terrible voice, but Juliet! Oh, Harry, she was about seventeen, with dark brown hair and a face like a flower. She was the loveliest girl that I'd ever seen in my life, and her voice was like music. I love her, Harry. She's everything to me. Every night I go to see her in different plays and she's always wonderful.'

'That's the reason, I suppose, why you never have dinner with me now,' said Lord Henry.

'But Harry, you and I see each other every day – we always have lunch together,' said Dorian in surprise. 'I have to go and see Sybil in the theatre every night. You and Basil must come with me to see her. Then you can see yourself how wonderful she is. Come tomorrow.'

'Very well, my dear Dorian, we'll come and watch your Juliet. But you'll be in love many times, you know – this is only the beginning.'

After Dorian had gone, Lord Henry smiled to himself. How amusing it was to watch this young man, he thought. He was very different now from the frightened boy in Basil Hallward's house. He had opened like a flower in the sun, and was learning to enjoy every pleasure in life. 'And it is I,' thought Lord Henry, 'who have taught him how to do this.'

When Lord Henry returned home that night, there was a letter for him lying on the table. It told him that Dorian Gray was going to marry Sybil Vane.

7

'Mother, Mother, I'm so happy,' cried the girl, 'and you must be happy too.'

Mrs Vane put her thin white hands on her daughter's head. 'I'm only happy when I see you in the theatre,' she said. 'And we are poor. We need the money – don't forget that. What do we know about this young man? You don't know his real name, or anything about him.'

'No, but I call him Prince Charming. He's everything to me. I love him and he loves me. Oh Mother, let me be happy!'

'You're too young to think of love,' said her mother. She looked at her daughter's lovely face, and tried to warn her of the dangers of love, but the girl did not listen. She was locked in her prison of love.

At that moment the girl's brother entered the room. He was a heavy, dark young man, not at all like his sister.

'I've heard about a gentleman who visits you every night at the theatre,' he said to his sister. 'Who is he? What does he want?'

'Oh James, don't be angry with me today,' cried Sybil. 'You're leaving for Australia tomorrow, and today is your last day. Come for a walk with me in the park. I'll go and get ready.' She danced out of the room, and her mother and brother could hear her singing as she ran upstairs.

James Vane turned to his mother. 'My new life as a sailor will keep me away from England for many years,' he said. 'But I don't like to leave Sybil alone.'

'Sybil has me, her mother, you know,' said Mrs Vane quietly.

'Oh James, don't be angry with me today,' cried Sybil Vane.

'Then take care of her.' James Vane gave his mother a long, hard look. 'If that man hurts my sister, I'll find him, and kill him like a dog.'

8

As they waited for Dorian Gray the next night, Lord Henry and Basil Hallward discussed Sybil Vane. Basil had not been happy at the news of Dorian's marriage plans.

'An actress!' he had cried. 'But Dorian is a gentleman, the grandson of Lord Kelso. He can't marry an actress.'

'Why not?' Lord Henry had said coolly. 'He'll love her wildly for six months, and then suddenly he'll be in love with another woman. It will be very amusing to watch.'

But when Dorian arrived and told the story of his love, Basil became a little happier. 'You're right,' he told Dorian. 'The woman that you love must be wonderful. I can see already that she's changed you.'

'Yes,' said Dorian happily, 'yes, Sybil has changed me. From this moment I shall be good. I'll never listen again, Harry, to your dangerous ideas about life and pleasure.'

Lord Henry smiled. 'Ah,' he said, 'when we are happy, we are always good, but when we are good, we are not always happy.'

Basil Hallward shook his head at this, but Dorian laughed. 'You cut life to pieces with your clever words, Harry.'

The theatre was crowded and noisy, but when Sybil Vane

appeared, everyone became silent. She was one of the most beautiful girls that Lord Henry had ever seen. 'Lovely! Lovely!' he said softly.

But although Sybil looked beautiful, her voice sounded unnatural. She spoke Juliet's words, but there was no feeling in them. Her voice was lovely, but it took away all the life from the words. People in the theatre began talking loudly, and after half an hour Lord Henry stood up and put on his coat.

'She's very beautiful, Dorian, but she's not an actress,' he said. 'Let's go.'

'I think that Miss Vane must be ill,' added Basil. 'We'll come another night.'

Dorian did not look at them. 'Go away. I want to be alone,' he said miserably, and as his friends left, he covered his face with his hands.

When the play came to its painful end, Dorian went to see Sybil.

'I wasn't a very good Juliet tonight,' she said, and looked at him with love in her eyes.

'You were terrible,' said Dorian coldly. 'My friends were bored. I was bored. I suppose you were ill.'

She did not seem to hear him. 'Dorian,' she cried, 'before I knew you, the theatre was my only life. I thought that it was all true. I knew nothing but shadows, and I thought that they were real. But you've taught me the difference between art and life. How can I pretend to be Juliet – to feel Juliet's love, when I know now what true love is?'

Dorian turned his face away from her. 'But I loved you for your art – because you were a wonderful actress,' he said. His voice was hard. 'You have killed my love. Without your art, you are nothing. I never want to see you again.'

Sybil's face was white with fear. 'You're not serious, are you, Dorian?' she asked. She touched his arm with her small, gentle hand.

'Don't touch me!' he shouted angrily. He pushed her away, and she fell to the floor and lay there like a broken bird.

'Dorian, please don't leave me,' she cried. 'I love you better than anything in the world. Don't leave me!'

'I love you better than anything in the world.
Don't leave me, Dorian!'

Dorian Gray looked down at her with his beautiful eyes. There was no love or gentleness in his face. 'I'm going,' he said at last. 'I don't wish to be unkind, but I don't want to see you again.' Without another word he left her.

All night he walked through the streets of London. When morning came, he went home. When he entered his house, he saw the portrait of himself that Basil Hallward had painted. There was something different about it, he thought. The face had changed – there was something unkind, and cruel about the mouth. It was very strange.

He picked up a mirror and looked at his own face, and then looked again at the face in the portrait. Yes, it *was* different. What did this change mean?

Suddenly he remembered his wish in Basil Hallward's house . . . his wish that he could stay young, but the picture could grow old. The idea was impossible, of course. But why did the face in the picture have that cruel, unkind mouth?

Cruel! Had he been cruel to Sybil Vane? He remembered her white, unhappy face as she lay at his feet. But she had hurt him, too. No, Sybil Vane was nothing to him now.

But the picture watched him, with its beautiful face and its cruel smile. It had taught him to love his own beauty. Would it also teach him to hate his own heart, his own soul? No, he would go back to Sybil Vane. He would marry her, try to love her again. Poor child! How cruel he had been to her! They would be happy together.

He covered the picture and quickly left the room.

The Death of Love

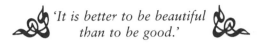

'It is better to be beautiful than to be good.'

9

I t was long past midday when Dorian woke up. His servant brought him tea and his letters, but he did not read them. Yesterday seemed like a bad dream, but when he went downstairs, he saw the covered picture. Should he uncover it, he wondered? Had the face in the picture really changed? Did he want to know? He lit a cigarette and thought for a while. Yes, he had to know. He lifted the cover.

There was no mistake. The portrait had really changed. He could not explain it, could not understand it. It was impossible, but it had happened.

Dorian felt sick and ashamed. He did not know what to do, or what to think. Finally, he sat down and wrote a long letter to Sybil Vane. He covered page after page with wild words of love. Then, suddenly, he heard Lord Henry's voice at the door. Dorian jumped up and covered the picture.

'My dear boy,' said Lord Henry, as he came in. 'I'm so sorry. But you must not think too much about her.'

'Do you mean about Sybil Vane?' asked Dorian. 'There's nothing to be sorry about. I want to be good, and I'm going to be happy. I shall marry Sybil Vane. I'm not going to break my promise to her.'

'Marry Sybil Vane!' Lord Henry stared at Dorian. 'Didn't you get my letter?'

*The portrait had really changed. There was something unkind,
and cruel about the mouth. It was very strange.*

'I haven't read my letters today,' said Dorian slowly.

Lord Henry walked across the room and took Dorian's hands in his own. 'Dorian,' he said quietly, 'don't be frightened – my letter told you that Sybil Vane is dead. She killed herself at the theatre last night.'

'No, no, that's impossible!' cried Dorian. He pulled his hands away and stared at Lord Henry with wild eyes. 'This is terrible, Harry. I have murdered Sybil Vane!'

'She killed herself,' said Lord Henry calmly. 'You didn't murder her. She killed herself because she loved you. It's very sad, of course, but you mustn't think too much about it. You must come and have dinner with me.'

'Harry, listen. Last night I told her that I didn't want to see her again. But after I left her, I realized how cruel I had been. I decided to go back to her, to marry her. And now she is dead! Harry, what shall I do? You don't know the danger that I am in.'

'My dear Dorian,' said Lord Henry. 'Marriage with Sybil Vane was not for you. No, no . . . marriages like that are never successful. The man quickly becomes unhappy and bored. Of course, he's kind to his wife. We can always be kind to people that we're not interested in. But the woman soon discovers that her husband is bored. And then she either becomes terribly unfashionable, or wears very expensive hats that another woman's husband has to pay for.'

The young man walked up and down the room. 'I suppose that's true,' he said unhappily. 'But Harry, I don't think that I'm cruel. Do you?'

Lord Henry smiled. He told Dorian Gray what he wanted to hear. And then he told him clever, amusing stories about the women that he himself had loved. He said that Sybil Vane's death was a beautiful end to a love story for an actress. 'The girl never really lived,' he continued, 'so she never really died. Don't cry for Sybil Vane. She was less real than Juliet.'

After a while Dorian Gray looked up. 'You have explained me to myself, Harry,' he said slowly. 'How well you know me! But we won't talk of this again. It's been a wonderful lesson for me. That's all.'

When Lord Henry had left, Dorian uncovered the picture again. He had to choose between a good life and a bad life, he thought. But then he realized that, in fact, he had already chosen. He would stay young for ever, and enjoy every wild pleasure that life could give him. The face in the picture would grow old and ugly and unkind, but he would stay beautiful for ever. He covered the picture again, and smiled.

An hour later he was at Lord Henry's house, and Lord Henry was smiling at his side.

10

While Dorian was having breakfast the next morning, Basil Hallward came to see him.

'At last I've found you, Dorian,' he said seriously. 'I came last night, but they told me that you'd gone out to dinner with friends. I knew that wasn't true, of course. I wanted to tell you how sorry I was about Sybil Vane. Poor girl!'

'My dear Basil,' said Dorian. He looked bored. 'I was at

Lord Henry's house last night. It was a very amusing evening.'

Basil stared at him. 'You went out to dinner?' he said slowly. 'You went out to dinner when Sybil Vane was lying dead in some dirty theatre?'

'Stop, Basil! I won't listen to you!' Dorian jumped to his feet. 'Sybil Vane is in the past . . . finished . . . forgotten.'

'You went out to dinner when Sybil Vane was lying dead in some dirty theatre?' asked Basil.

'You've changed, Dorian,' said Basil. 'You have the same wonderful face, but where is the kind and gentle boy who sat for my portrait? Have you no heart?'

'Yesterday my heart was full of sadness. I have cried for Sybil, yes, but I cannot cry today. I *have* changed, Basil. I'm a man now, with new feelings, new ideas. Don't be angry with me. I am what I am. There's nothing more to say.'

Basil watched him sadly. 'Well, Dorian,' he said at last, 'I won't speak of poor Sybil again. But will you come and sit for another portrait soon?'

'No. Never,' said Dorian quickly. 'It's impossible.'

'But why?' asked Basil, very surprised. 'And why have you covered the portrait?' He walked across the room towards the painting.

Dorian cried out in fear, and ran between Basil and the portrait. 'No, Basil! You must not look at it. I don't want you to see it.' His face was white and angry. 'If you try to look at it, I'll never speak to you again.'

The artist stared at him. 'Why can't I look at my own work?' he asked. 'I'm going to exhibit it in an art gallery in Paris soon.'

Dorian tried to hide his fear. 'But you said . . . you told me that you would never exhibit the picture. Why have you changed your mind?' He came closer to Basil and looked into his face. 'Tell me why,' he said.

Basil turned away. After a while he said slowly, 'I see that you too have noticed something strange about the picture. Dorian, you changed my life as an artist from the moment when I met you. You became very important to me – I could not stop thinking about you. And when I painted this portrait, I felt that I'd put too much of myself into it. I could not let other people see it.' He was silent for a moment, then turned back to Dorian. 'Perhaps you're right. I cannot exhibit this picture. But will you let me look at it again?'

'No, never!'

The artist smiled sadly. 'Well, I've told you my secret now. Try to understand me, Dorian. You've been the one person in my life who has really influenced my art.'

As he left the room, Dorian Gray smiled to himself. What a dangerous moment that had been! Poor Basil! Although he had told his own secret, he had not discovered Dorian's secret. But the picture . . . he must hide it away at once. No one must ever see it again.

He had the covered portrait carried upstairs to a small room at the top of the house. Then he locked the door and kept the key himself. He felt safe now, because only his eyes would see the terrible changes in that beautiful face.

When he returned to the room downstairs, he picked up a book that Lord Henry had lent him. He sat down and began to read.

It was the story of a Frenchman, who had spent his life searching for beauty and pleasure – pleasure of all kinds, both good and bad. Dorian read for hours. It was a frightening book, full of strange ideas and dangerous dreams – dreams that slowly became real for Dorian.

Dorian read this book many times. In fact, he could not stop reading it, and over the years, it became more and more interesting to him. He felt that the Frenchman's life was a mirror of his own.

The Thief of Time

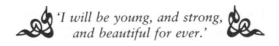
'I will be young, and strong, and beautiful for ever.'

11

And so the years passed.

But time did not touch the face of Dorian Gray. That wonderful beauty – the beauty that Basil Hallward had painted – never left him. He enjoyed the life of a rich and fashionable young man. He studied art and music, and filled his house with beautiful things from every corner of the world. But his search for pleasure did not stop there. He became hungry for evil pleasures. He became more and more in love with the beauty of his face, more and more interested in the ugliness of his soul.

After a while strange stories were heard about him – stories of a secret, more dangerous life. But when people looked at that young and good-looking face, they could not believe the evil stories. And they still came to the famous dinners at his house, where the food, and the music, and the conversation were the best in London.

But behind the locked door at the top of the house, the picture of Dorian Gray grew older every year. The terrible face showed the dark secrets of his life. The heavy mouth, the yellow skin, the cruel eyes – these told the real story. Again and again, Dorian Gray went secretly to the room and looked first at the ugly and terrible face in the picture, then at the beautiful young face that laughed back at him from the mirror.

As time passed, the face in the picture grew slowly more terrible.

After his twenty-fifth year, the stories about him became worse. He was sometimes away from home for several days; he was seen fighting with foreign sailors in bars; he was friendly with thieves. And in the houses of fashionable people, men sometimes turned away when he entered a room. Women's faces sometimes went white when they heard his name.

But many people only laughed at these stories. Dorian Gray was still a very rich and fashionable man, and the dinners at his house were excellent. People agreed with Lord Henry, who once said, in his amusing way, that a good dinner was more important than a good life.

As the months and years passed, Dorian Gray grew more and more afraid of the picture. He both hated it and loved it, and he became more and more afraid that someone would discover his secret. For weeks he tried not to go near it, but he could not stay away from it for long. Sometimes, when he was staying in friends' houses, he suddenly left and hurried back to London. He wanted to be sure that the room was still locked and the picture was still safe. At one time he used to spend winters with Lord Henry in a little house in Algiers, but now he no longer travelled outside England.

His fear grew stronger every year, and as time passed, the face in the picture grew slowly more terrible.

The Hand of a Killer

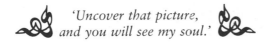

12

It was the ninth of November, the evening before his thirty-eighth birthday. Dorian Gray was walking home from Lord Henry's house when he saw Basil Hallward. He felt strangely afraid and tried to pretend that he had not seen him, but Basil hurried after him.

'Dorian!' he called. 'What extraordinary luck! I'm catching the midnight train to Paris and I wanted to see you before I left. I'll be away from England for six months.' He put his hand on Dorian's arm. 'Look, we're near your house. May I come in for a moment? I have something to say to you.'

'Of course. But won't you miss your train?' asked Dorian lazily, as he walked up the steps to his door.

'I have plenty of time. It's only eleven o'clock.'

They went in and sat down by the fire.

'Now, my dear Dorian, I want to speak to you seriously,' Basil began. 'I must tell you that people in London are saying the most terrible things about you.'

Dorian lit a cigarette and looked bored. 'I don't want to know anything about it. It doesn't interest me.'

'But it must interest you, Dorian,' said Basil. 'Every gentleman is interested in his good name. Of course, when I look at you, I know that these stories can't be true. A man's face shows if his life is good or bad. But why does Lord Berwick leave the room when you enter it? Why does Lord Staveley say that no honest woman is safe with you? That young soldier, who was your friend – why did he kill himself? There was Sir Henry Ashton, who had to leave England with a bad name. And what about Lord Kent's son? What kind of life does he have now?'

'Stop, Basil. You don't know what you're talking about,' said Dorian coldly. 'Did I teach these people how to live their lives? And the people who tell these stories – are their lives any better than mine?'

'And there are other stories too,' continued Basil. 'Are they true? Can your life really be so bad, so evil? You were a fine young man once, but now, when I hear these stories, I wonder . . . Do I know you at all? What has happened to the real Dorian Gray? I think I would have to see your soul before I could answer those questions.'

'The real Dorian Gray?' asked Dorian quietly, his face white with fear.

'Yes,' said the artist sadly. 'But only God can see your soul.'

A terrible laugh came from the younger man. 'Come, Basil,' he cried. 'Come with me! I will show you what only God can see. Why not? It's your own work. You've talked enough about evil. Now you must look at it.'

He took Basil upstairs to the locked room. Inside, he turned to the artist, with smiling lips and cold, hard eyes. 'You're the one man in the world who *should* know my secret. Are you sure that you want to?'

'Yes.'

'Then uncover that picture, Basil, and you will see my soul.'

A cry of horror came from the artist when he saw the terrible face in the portrait. How could that evil and unlovely face be Dorian Gray's? But yes, it was. He went nearer to the picture. It could not be the portrait that he had painted. But yes, there was his name written in the corner. He turned and looked at Dorian Gray with the eyes of a sick man.

'What does this mean?' he asked at last.

'When you finished the portrait,' replied Dorian, 'I made a wish . . .'

'I remember, yes,' said Basil. 'You wished that the picture could become old, and that you could stay young. But this . . .' He stared again at the picture. 'This is impossible. And you told me that you'd destroyed the picture.'

'I was wrong. It has destroyed me.'

'My God, Dorian!' cried the artist. 'If this is true . . . If this is the face of your soul, then you are more evil than the worst of the stories about you.' He sat down at the table and put his face in his hands. 'You must ask God for his help.'

'It's too late, Basil.'

'It's never too late, Dorian. Look at that terrible face. Look at it!'

Dorian turned and stared at the face in the picture, and suddenly he hated Basil more than he had ever hated anyone in his life. Basil now knew his secret, and had seen the real Dorian Gray. Violent feelings burned inside Dorian. He picked up a knife from the table. Then the hate inside him exploded, and like a wild animal, he ran towards Basil, and dug the knife into the artist's neck, again and again and

Dorian stood and listened. He could hear nothing —
only the drip, drip of blood onto the floor.

again. The murdered man's head fell forwards, and the blood ran slowly across the table, and down onto the floor.

Dorian stood and listened. He could hear nothing – only the drip, drip of blood onto the floor. He went to the window and looked down into the street. He felt strangely calm. The friend who had painted his portrait had gone out of his life. That was all.

He locked the door behind him and went quietly downstairs. His servants were all in bed. He sat down and began to think. No one had seen Basil in Dorian's house tonight. Paris. Yes! Basil had gone to Paris, of course, so it would be six months before people asked where he was. Six months! That was more than enough time.

Dorian walked up and down the room. Then he took out a book from his desk and began to search for a name. Alan Campbell. Yes, that was the name that he wanted.

13

The next morning Dorian wrote two letters. He put one of them into his pocket, and he gave the other to his servant. 'Take this to Mr Campbell's house at once,' he said.

While Dorian waited, he picked up a book and tried to read. But after a time the book fell from his hand. Perhaps Alan Campbell was out of England. Perhaps he would refuse to come. He was a very clever scientist, and five years ago he and Dorian had been good friends. But now Alan never smiled when he met Dorian.

Each minute seemed an hour to Dorian, but at last the door opened. Dorian smiled. 'Alan!' he said. 'Thank you for coming.'

'I never wanted to enter your house again, but your letter said that it was a question of life and death,' said Alan Campbell. His voice was hard and cold.

'Yes, Alan, it is. Please sit down.' Across the table the two men's eyes met. Dorian was silent for a moment; then, very quietly, he said, 'Alan, in a locked room upstairs there is a dead body. I want you to destroy it. There must be nothing left. I know you can do this.'

'Alan, in a locked room upstairs there is a dead body.
I want you to destroy it.'

'I don't want to know your terrible secrets. I refuse to help you,' Campbell replied.

'But you must, Alan. You're the only person who can help me.' Dorian smiled sadly. He took a piece of paper, wrote something on it, and pushed it across the table to Campbell.

As Campbell read the piece of paper, his face went white. He looked at Dorian with hate and fear in his eyes.

'I'm so sorry for you, Alan,' said Dorian gently. 'I've already written a letter, and if you don't help me, I'll have to send it. But I think that you *will* help me.'

Campbell put his face in his hands, and was silent for a long time. Dorian waited.

'I'll need some things from my house,' Campbell said at last.

Dorian sent his servant to fetch the things that Campbell needed, and the two men waited silently. When the servant returned, Dorian took the scientist upstairs to the locked room. As they entered, Dorian remembered that the portrait was uncovered. He turned to cover it, then stopped and stared in horror. One of the hands in the picture was red with blood. For Dorian, this was more terrible than the dead body in the room. With shaking hands, he quickly covered the picture.

'Leave me now,' ordered Campbell.

Five hours later Campbell came back downstairs. 'I've done what you asked me to do,' he said. 'And now goodbye. I never want to see you again.'

When Campbell had left, Dorian went upstairs. There was a terrible smell in the room, but the dead body had gone.

The Sailor

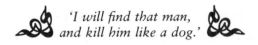

*'I will find that man,
and kill him like a dog.'*

14

ater the same evening Dorian Gray was at a party. He smiled and talked, and looked as young and as good-looking as ever. But his head ached and at dinner he could not eat anything. When Lord Henry asked him if he felt unwell, Dorian said that he was tired and would go home early.

At home he felt worse. Although the room was warm, his hands shook with cold. He wanted to forget for a while – to escape from the prison of his real life, and to lose himself in dreams.

At midnight, in old dirty clothes, he left the house again and went to the East End of London. There he knew places where he could get opium – dark, evil places where people bought and sold the beautiful, terrible dreams of opium. He had been there many times before.

He found the house that he was looking for and went into a long, low room. Men were lying on the dirty floor, a sailor was asleep on a table and two women were drinking at the bar. As Dorian hurried up the narrow stairs, the sweet, heavy smell of opium came to meet him and he smiled in pleasure. But in the room he saw a young man who had once been his friend. He turned away, and went downstairs again to drink at the bar.

One of the women spoke to him.

'Don't talk to me,' said Dorian angrily, and walked towards the door.

'I remember you! You're Prince Charming, aren't you?' she shouted after him.

The sleeping sailor woke up when he heard these words, and as Dorian left the house, the sailor hurried after him.

Dorian walked quickly along the road, but as he reached a corner, hands closed around his neck. A man pulled him backwards and pushed him against a wall. Dorian fought wildly, and pulled the hands away. Then he saw the gun in the man's hand.

'What do you want?' he said quickly.

'Keep quiet,' said the man. 'If you move, I'll shoot you.'

'You're crazy. What have I done to you?'

'You destroyed the life of Sybil Vane,' answered the sailor, 'and Sybil Vane was my sister. She killed herself because of you. I've been looking for you for years, but I only knew the name that she used to call you – Prince Charming. Well, tonight I heard your name, and tonight you're going to die.'

Dorian Gray grew sick with fear. 'I never knew her. I've never heard of her. You're crazy,' he cried. Suddenly he had an idea. 'How long ago did your sister die?' he asked.

'Eighteen years ago,' James Vane replied. 'Why do you ask me?'

'Eighteen years,' laughed Dorian Gray. 'Take me to the light and look at my face.'

James Vane stared at Dorian. Then he pushed him towards the light, and in the light he saw the face of a boy of twenty.

'I've been looking for you for years – Prince Charming!'
said James Vane.

This man was too young. He was not the man who had destroyed his sister's life.

'My God!' he cried. 'I nearly murdered you!'

'Go home, and put that gun away, before you get into trouble,' said Dorian. And he walked quickly away.

James Vane stared after him in horror. Then a woman's hand touched his arm.

'Why didn't you kill him?' she asked. 'He's evil.'

'He's not the man that I'm looking for,' answered the sailor. 'The man who I want must be nearly forty now. That man is only a boy.'

'A boy?' The woman laughed. Her voice was hard. 'It's eighteen years since I met Prince Charming. And his pretty face hasn't changed in all that time. It's true, I promise you.'

James Vane ran to the corner of the road, but Dorian Gray had disappeared.

15

A week later Dorian Gray was at his house in the country, where he had invited Lord Henry and several other friends. Among them was the pretty Lady Monmouth and her much older husband. Lady Monmouth was amusing and clever, and seemed to like Dorian Gray very much. One afternoon, as they laughed and talked together during tea, Dorian went out to fetch a flower for Lady Monmouth's dress. Lord Henry smiled at Lady Monmouth.

'I hope you're not in love with Dorian, my dear. He's very dangerous.'

She laughed. 'Oh, men are much more interesting when they're dangerous.'

Just then they heard the sound of a heavy fall. Lord Henry ran out of the room and found Dorian lying unconscious on the floor. When Dorian opened his eyes, Lord Henry said, 'My dear Dorian, you must take care of yourself. You're not well.'

Dorian stood up slowly. 'I'm all right, Harry. I'm all right.'

As he dressed for dinner in his room, Dorian remembered what he had seen and cold fear ran through him like a knife. He had seen a face watching him at the window and he had recognized it. It was the face of James Vane.

The next day he did not leave the house. In fact, for most of the day he stayed in his room, sick with fear. Every time he closed his eyes, he saw again the sailor's face. He tried to tell himself that he had dreamt it. Yes, it was impossible. Sybil Vane's brother did not know his name, and was probably on his ship at sea. No, of course he had not seen James Vane's face at the window.

But the fear stayed with him, dream or no dream.

Two days passed and Dorian grew less afraid. On the third day, a clear, bright winter morning, Dorian joined his friends on a shooting-party. With Lady Monmouth by his side, he walked to the edge of the forest where the men were shooting at birds and small animals. The cold air and the sounds and smells of the forest filled Dorian with happiness. Suddenly one of the men shot into the trees near them. There were two cries in the morning air – the cry of an animal and the cry of a man, both in pain.

There were shouts and calls from the men, and then a man's body was pulled from the trees. Dorian turned away in horror. Bad luck seemed to follow him everywhere.

A man's dead body was pulled from the trees.

People began to walk back towards the house. Lord Henry came over to tell Dorian that the man was dead.

Dorian shook his head. 'Oh, Harry,' he said slowly, 'I feel that something terrible is going to happen to some of us – to me, perhaps.'

Lord Henry laughed at this idea. 'What could happen to you, Dorian? You have everything in the world that a man can want. Forget about this accident. It was just an accident – not murder.' Then he added with a smile, 'But it would be very interesting to meet a person who *had* murdered somebody.'

'What a terrible thing to say!' cried Lady Monmouth. 'Don't you agree, Mr Gray? Mr Gray! Are you ill again? Your face is so white!'

Dorian smiled and tried to speak calmly. 'It's nothing,' he said quietly. 'But please excuse me. I think I must go and lie down.'

Upstairs in his room Dorian's body shook with fear like a leaf in the wind. He felt that he could not stay another night in the house. Death walked there in the sunlight. He decided to return immediately to London and to visit his doctor. His servant came to pack his clothes, and while he was doing this, he told Dorian that the dead man was a sailor, but no one knew his name.

'A sailor!' cried Dorian. He jumped to his feet. A wild hope filled him. 'I must see the body at once.'

He hurried to the house where the body lay, and when he uncovered the face of the dead man, he saw that it was James Vane. He cried with happiness, and knew that now he was safe.

The Picture

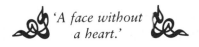 *'A face without a heart.'*

16

'Y'ou're going to be good?' said Lord Henry. 'Don't tell me that. You're wonderful as you are. Please don't change.' His long, white fingers played with a flower on the table. It was spring in London, and the two friends were having dinner at Lord Henry's house.

Dorian Gray shook his head. 'No, Harry, I've done too many terrible things in my life, and I'm going to change. I began my good life yesterday, in the country.'

'My dear boy,' smiled Lord Henry. 'Everybody can be good in the country. There's nothing to do in the country, so it's impossible to do anything bad. But tell me, how did you begin your good life?'

'There was a girl in a village. A very beautiful girl, an honest, country girl. She loved me, and was ready to come away with me yesterday, but I said no. I refused to destroy her young life, and I've left her as honest as I found her.'

Lord Henry laughed. 'You've left her with a broken heart, you mean. How can she be happy now with a country boy, after she has known you?'

'Don't, Harry!' cried Dorian. 'Can you never be serious? I'm sorry that I told you now. Let's talk about other things. What's been happening in London?'

'Oh, people are still discussing poor Basil and how he

disappeared. I don't know why, because there are plenty of other things that they can talk about – my wife has run away with another man, Alan Campbell has killed himself . . .'

'What do you think has happened to Basil?' asked Dorian slowly.

'I've no idea,' answered Lord Henry. 'The English police report that Basil went to Paris on the midnight train on the ninth of November, but the French police say that he never arrived in Paris at all. If Basil wants to hide himself, I really don't care. And if he's dead, I don't want to think about him. Death is the only thing that really frightens me – I hate it.'

'Harry, don't people say that . . . that Basil was murdered?' said Dorian.

'Some of the newspapers say so,' replied Lord Henry, 'but who would want to murder poor Basil? He wasn't clever enough to have enemies.'

'What will you say, Harry, if I tell you that *I* murdered Basil?' asked Dorian. He watched his friend carefully.

Lord Henry smiled. 'No, my dear Dorian, murder wouldn't please you. You like a different kind of pleasure. And you should never do anything that you cannot talk about after dinner.' He lifted his coffee cup. 'What happened to the fine portrait that Basil painted of you? I haven't seen it for years. Didn't you tell me that it was stolen? What a pity!'

'Oh, I never really liked it,' said Dorian. 'I prefer not to think about it.'

For a while the two men were silent. Then the older man lay back in his chair and looked at Dorian with half-closed eyes. 'Tell me how you have kept your youth and your wonderful beauty, Dorian. You must have some secret. I'm

'Tell me how you have kept your youth and your
wonderful beauty, Dorian,' said Lord Henry.

only ten years older than you, and I look like an old man. But you haven't changed since the day when I first met you. What a wonderful life you've had!'

'Yes,' said Dorian slowly, 'it's been wonderful, Harry, but I'm going to change it now. You don't know everything about me.'

His friend smiled. 'You cannot change to me, Dorian. You and I will always be friends.'

Dorian stood up. 'I'm tired tonight, Harry. I must go home. I'll see you at lunch tomorrow. Goodnight.'

At the door he stopped for a moment and looked back, but then he turned and went out without another word.

17

At home he thought about his conversation with Lord Henry. Could he really change, he wondered? He had lived an evil life, and had destroyed other people's lives as well. Was there any hope for him?

Why had he ever made that wish about the picture? He had kept his youth and beauty, but he had paid a terrible price for it. His beauty had destroyed his soul. He picked up a mirror and stared at his face. What was he now? A face without a heart. Suddenly he hated his own beauty, and dropped the mirror on the floor where it broke into many small pieces.

James Vane, Basil Hallward, Sybil Vane – these deaths were not important to him now. It was better not to think of the past. Nothing could change that. He must think of himself. 'Perhaps,' he thought, 'if I live a better life, the picture will become less ugly.' He remembered the pretty village girl – he had not destroyed her young life. He had done one good thing. Perhaps the picture had already begun to look better.

He went quietly upstairs to the locked room. Yes, he would live a good life, and he need not be afraid any more of the evil face of his soul. But when he uncovered the picture, he gave a cry of pain. There was no change. The face in the picture was still terrible – more hateful, if possible, than before – and the red on the hand seemed brighter, like new blood.

He stared at the picture with hate and fear in his eyes. Years ago he had loved to watch it changing and growing old; now he could not sleep because of it. It had stolen every chance of peace or happiness from him. He must destroy it.

He looked round and saw the knife that had killed Basil Hallward. 'Now it will kill the artist's work,' he said to himself. 'It will kill the past, and when that is dead, I will be free.' He picked up the knife and dug it into the picture.

There was a terrible cry, and a loud crash. The servants woke, and two gentlemen, who were passing in the road below, stopped and looked up at the house. A policeman came by, and they asked him:

'Whose house is that?'

'Mr Dorian Gray's, sir,' was the answer.

The two gentlemen looked at each other, then turned away from the house and walked on.

Inside the house the servants talked in low, frightened voices. After some minutes they went up to the room. They knocked, but there was no reply. They called out. Nothing.

Lying on the floor was a dead man, with a knife in his heart.

They could not open the door, so they climbed down from the roof and got in through the window.

Against the wall they saw a fine portrait of the young Dorian Gray, in all his wonderful youth and beauty. Lying on the floor was a dead man, with a knife in his heart. His face was old and ugly and yellow with disease.

Only the rings on his fingers told them who he was.

GLOSSARY

art making beautiful things, e.g. pictures and paintings; cleverness at doing things, e.g. acting

artist somebody who paints or draws pictures

art gallery a building where people go to look at famous paintings

aunt the sister of your father or mother

beauty being beautiful

believe to think that something is true or right

cruel very unkind; giving unhappiness to other people

evil very, very bad

exhibit to show something to people, e.g. to put pictures in an art gallery for people to look at (and perhaps buy)

gentleman (in this story) a man of good family, usually rich

God the 'person' who made the world and controls all things

Harry a different form of the name Henry

horror a feeling of very strong fear, dislike, and surprise

influence *(v)* to change someone or something; make someone do what you want

Lord a title ('Dr', 'Mrs' are titles) for a man from an old and important family

marriage the time when a man and a woman are married

opium a drug made from flowers that makes people sleep

paint *(v)* to make a picture with colours

paradise a place (not real) where people are completely happy

play *(n)* a story that people act in a theatre

pleasure the feeling of being happy and doing things that you like

portrait a painting or picture of a person

Prince Charming the kind of rich and good-looking man that young girls dream about

scent *(n)* a sweet, lovely smell

scientist someone who studies science, which is the study of natural things, e.g. biology, chemistry, physics

servant someone who works in another person's house

sit (for a picture) to sit or stand while an artist paints a picture of you

sitter a person that an artist is painting

soul the part of a person that is not the body

stare to look hard and long at something or somebody

ugly not beautiful; not pleasing to look at

unconscious not knowing what is happening; in a kind of sleep caused by illness or a hit on the head

youth being young

ACTIVITIES

Before Reading

1 **Read the story introduction on the first page of the book and the back cover. How much do you know now about the story? For each sentence, circle Y (Yes) or N (No).**

1 Lord Henry thinks that it is important to be good. Y/N
2 Someone paints a picture of Dorian Gray. Y/N
3 Dorian Gray is a beautiful young woman. Y/N
4 Dorian Gray wants to be beautiful all his life. Y/N
5 Dorian Gray's face becomes old and ugly. Y/N
6 The painter of the portrait hated Dorian Gray. Y/N

2 **What is going to happen in the story? Can you guess? For each sentence, circle Y (Yes) or N (No).**

1 Lord Henry changes Dorian Gray's life. Y/N
2 Dorian Gray kills someone. Y/N
3 Lord Henry kills Dorian Gray. Y/N
4 A woman falls in love with Dorian Gray. Y/N
5 Dorian Gray gets married. Y/N
6 Dorian Gray sells the painting. Y/N
7 Dorian Gray destroys the painting. Y/N
8 The painter tries to help Dorian Gray. Y/N

ACTIVITIES

While Reading

Read Chapters 1 and 2, and then answer these questions.

Why

1 ... didn't Basil Hallward want to exhibit the portrait?
2 ... did Basil prefer not to be beautiful?
3 ... did Basil now see art in a different way?
4 ... didn't Basil want Lord Henry to meet Dorian?

Read Chapters 3 to 5. Who said this, and to whom?

1 'I'm afraid I must ask you to go away.'
2 'I'd like you to talk to me.'
3 'You have a wonderfully beautiful face ...'
4 'It's your best work.'
5 'I wish the picture could change, and I could stay as I am.'
6 'You're my dearest friend.'

Read Chapters 6 to 8. Are these sentences true (T) or false (F)? Rewrite the false ones with the correct information.

1 Dorian fell in love with an actress called Sybil Vane.
2 Sybil Vane's family was rich.
3 James Vane didn't worry about his sister and Dorian.
4 Lord Henry thought that Sybil was a good actress.
5 Dorian loved Sybil for her beauty.
6 Dorian said that he never wanted to see Sybil again.

Before you read Chapters 9 and 10 (*The Death of Love*), can you guess what happens? Choose one of these answers.

1 Sybil and Dorian get married and are very happy.
2 Sybil and Dorian get married and are very unhappy.
3 Sybil runs away to her brother in Australia.
4 Sybil kills herself and Dorian doesn't care.
5 Sybil kills herself and Dorian is very sorry.

Read Chapter 11. Use these words to complete this paragraph about Dorian Gray. Then find words in the chapter that mean the opposite of the words given.

beauty, dangerous, evil, good-looking, loved, terrible, ugly, young

Dorian Gray was in love with the _____ of his face. Strange stories were told about his secret, _____ life. But people did not believe the _____ stories because Dorian's face was _____ and _____. The portrait was the only thing that showed the real Dorian. It became more and more _____ and _____, and Dorian grew more and more afraid of it, but he _____ it too.

Read Chapters 12 and 13. Choose the best question-word for these questions and then answer them.

How / What / Where / Why
1 . . . was Basil going?
2 . . . had Basil heard about Dorian?
3 . . . did Dorian take Basil?
4 . . . did Basil feel when he saw the picture?

5 . . . did Dorian hate Basil?

6 . . . did Basil die?

7 . . . did Alan Campbell feel about Dorian?

8 . . . did Dorian want Alan to do?

9 . . . did Alan agree to help Dorian?

10 . . . did Dorian see when he looked at the picture?

Before you read Chapters 14 and 15 (*The Sailor*), can you guess what happens? For each sentence, circle Y (yes) or N (No).

1 James Vane comes back and finds Dorian. Y/N

2 James Vane tries to shoot Dorian. Y/N

3 Dorian runs away to America because he is afraid of James Vane. Y/N

4 Dorian kills James Vane. Y/N

Read Chapters 16 and 17, and then answer these questions.

1 How did Dorian try to change his life?

2 Why didn't Lord Henry want to think about Basil?

3 What was the difference between Lord Henry and Dorian?

4 What did Dorian see when he looked in the mirror?

5 Why did he break the mirror?

6 What did Dorian hope had happened to the picture?

7 Why did he dig a knife into the picture?

8 How did people recognize Dorian when he was dead?

ACTIVITIES

After Reading

1 Complete this conversation between James Vane and his mother, after his return from Australia. Use as many words as you like.

JAMES VANE: What really happened to Sybil, mother?

MRS VANE: I told you in my letter. _____.

JAMES VANE: But why did she kill herself? It was because of that man, wasn't it?

MRS VANE: Yes, _____.

JAMES VANE: When did this happen?

MRS VANE: _____.

JAMES VANE: So soon! What did he do to her? Do you know?

MRS VANE: Yes, I do. She left me a note. He _____.

JAMES VANE: I knew that he was dangerous, but why did he get tired of her so quickly?

MRS VANE: He said _____.

JAMES VANE: So she had nothing to live for! Well, I promise I won't rest until I've killed him. He is an evil man. What was his name?

MRS VANE: I don't know. But _____.

JAMES VANE: Well, I'll look for this 'Prince Charming' and make him sorry that he destroyed my sister.

MRS VANE: Oh, James, _____.

JAMES VANE: Don't worry, mother. I've got a gun.

2 **Here is the story that Dorian's servants told the police. Fill in the gaps with these words.**

angry, beautiful, door, floor, frightened, heard, knocked, locked, loud, old, portrait, reply, rings, roof, room, top, ugly, wall, window, woke

We _____ up in the middle of the night because we _____ a terrible cry and a _____ crash. The noise seemed to come from the _____ room at the _____ of the house. We were very _____ , and we didn't know what to do. Mr Gray never let us go into that _____ and we were afraid that he would be _____ with us if we opened the door. So we _____ and called his name, but there was no _____ . Then we tried to open the _____ , but it was locked, so we climbed out onto the _____ , and then got down into the locked room through the _____ . It was terrible! There was a wonderful _____ of Mr Gray on the _____ ; he looked so young and _____ . But there was a dead man lying on the _____ . We didn't recognize him at first; he was _____ and yellow, his mouth was heavy and his eyes were cruel; it was the face of an evil, _____ man. But he had Mr Gray's _____ on his fingers, so we knew that it was him.

3 **Do you agree (A) or disagree (D) with these ideas about painting? Explain why.**

1 A painting can be more truthful than a photograph.
2 A portrait says more about the painter than the sitter.

4 Use the table to make as many sentences as you can about these people.

Dorian Gray / Basil Hallward / Henry Wotton / Sybil Vane / James Vane / Alan Campbell

_____ was a . . .

beautiful	artist		loved	
young	scientist		hated	himself
rich	gentleman	who	killed	herself
clever	actress		painted	
poor	man		was afraid of	_____
good	woman		was killed by	

Example: *James Vane* was a *young sailor* who *hated Dorian Gray.*

5 What did you think about the people in this story? Were they nice or nasty, clever or stupid? Who did you feel most sorry for? Choose some names from Activity 4, and complete some of these sentences.

1 I feel sorry for _____ because _____.

2 I think _____ was *right/wrong* to _____.

3 I think _____ did a very *bad/good* thing when _____.

4 I think _____ did a very *clever/stupid* thing when

   _____.

5 I think _____ was *stupider/nicer/nastier* than _____ because

   _____.

6 **Match these halves of sentences to make a paragraph about the portrait of Dorian Gray.**

1 Later, Basil wanted to exhibit the picture in Paris . . .
2 Basil then tried to destroy the portrait . . .
3 When Dorian first saw the portrait, . . .
4 He became angry and afraid . . .
5 Many years later, Basil finally saw the picture, . . .
6 As time passed, Dorian became more evil, . . .
7 The face in the picture began to change . . .

8 after Dorian had been cruel to Sybil Vane.
9 because the picture would stay young while he grew old.
10 he remembered Lord Henry's words about youth.
11 and so Dorian killed him.
12 but Dorian didn't let him see it.
13 although he knew that it was his best work.
14 and the face in the picture grew more and more terrible.

7 **Do you agree (A) or disagree (D) with these things that Lord Henry said? Explain why.**

1 'When we are happy, we are always good, but when we are good, we are not always happy.'
2 'And there's nothing more important, more valuable than beauty.'
3 'You should never do anything that you cannot talk about after dinner.'
4 'It's today that is important.'
5 'We can always be kind to people that we're not interested in.'

ABOUT THE AUTHOR

Oscar Wilde was born in Dublin in 1854. He went to college there and then continued his studies in Oxford, where in 1878 he won a poetry prize. In 1882, his first book of poems was published and the next year he went to the USA to give talks. In 1884, he got married, and in 1888 he wrote a book of stories for his sons, *The Happy Prince and Other Tales*. He wrote other books of stories, but *The Picture of Dorian Gray* (1890) was his only novel. When it appeared, many people were angry, saying that it was a bad book with evil ideas. But Wilde did not agree that books could be bad or evil. 'Books are well written or badly written. That is all,' he wrote.

Wilde wrote his first play in 1883, but it was not successful, and neither was the next one. However, *Lady Windermere's Fan* (1892) was very popular with theatre-goers because of the clever words and the clear picture of people and the way they lived. Wilde's success continued until his greatest play, *The Importance of Being Earnest* (1895), but in that same year he was sent to prison because of his relationship with another man, Lord Alfred Douglas. When he came out in 1897, he went to live in France, where he wrote *The Ballad of Reading Gaol* (1898), a long poem about his experience of prison life. He died in Paris in 1900.

Today people still laugh at the clever things that Oscar Wilde said or wrote, but at the time some people did not think he was so clever. The painter Whistler was once talking to Wilde and said something amusing. Wilde said, 'I wish I had said that.' Whistler replied, 'You will, Oscar, you will.'

OXFORD BOOKWORMS LIBRARY

Classics • Crime & Mystery • Factfiles • Fantasy & Horror
Human Interest • Playscripts • Thriller & Adventure
True Stories • World Stories

The OXFORD BOOKWORMS LIBRARY provides enjoyable reading in English, with a wide range of classic and modern fiction, non-fiction, and plays. It includes original and adapted texts in seven carefully graded language stages, which take learners from beginner to advanced level. An overview is given on the next pages.

All Stage 1 titles are available as audio recordings, as well as over eighty other titles from Starter to Stage 6. All Starters and many titles at Stages 1 to 4 are specially recommended for younger learners. Every Bookworm is illustrated, and Starters and Factfiles have full-colour illustrations.

The OXFORD BOOKWORMS LIBRARY also offers extensive support. Each book contains an introduction to the story, notes about the author, a glossary, and activities. Additional resources include tests and worksheets, and answers for these and for the activities in the books. There is advice on running a class library, using audio recordings, and the many ways of using Oxford Bookworms in reading programmes. Resource materials are available on the website <www.oup.com/bookworms>.

The *Oxford Bookworms Collection* is a series for advanced learners. It consists of volumes of short stories by well-known authors, both classic and modern. Texts are not abridged or adapted in any way, but carefully selected to be accessible to the advanced student.

You can find details and a full list of titles in the *Oxford Bookworms Library Catalogue* and *Oxford English Language Teaching Catalogues*, and on the website <www.oup.com/bookworms>.

THE OXFORD BOOKWORMS LIBRARY
GRADING AND SAMPLE EXTRACTS

STARTER • 250 HEADWORDS
present simple – present continuous – imperative –
can/cannot, must – *going to* (future) – simple gerunds ...

Her phone is ringing – but where is it?

Sally gets out of bed and looks in her bag. No phone. She looks under the bed. No phone. Then she looks behind the door. There is her phone. Sally picks up her phone and answers it. *Sally's Phone*

STAGE 1 • 400 HEADWORDS
... past simple – coordination with *and, but, or* –
subordination with *before, after, when, because, so* ...

I knew him in Persia. He was a famous builder and I worked with him there. For a time I was his friend, but not for long. When he came to Paris, I came after him – I wanted to watch him. He was a very clever, very dangerous man. *The Phantom of the Opera*

STAGE 2 • 700 HEADWORDS
... present perfect – *will* (future) – *(don't) have to, must not, could* –
comparison of adjectives – simple *if* clauses – past continuous –
tag questions – *ask/tell* + infinitive ...

While I was writing these words in my diary, I decided what to do. I must try to escape. I shall try to get down the wall outside. The window is high above the ground, but I have to try. I shall take some of the gold with me – if I escape, perhaps it will be helpful later. *Dracula*

STAGE 3 • 1000 HEADWORDS

... should, may – present perfect continuous – *used to* – past perfect –
causative – relative clauses – indirect statements ...

Of course, it was most important that no one should see
Colin, Mary, or Dickon entering the secret garden. So Colin
gave orders to the gardeners that they must all keep away
from that part of the garden in future. *The Secret Garden*

STAGE 4 • 1400 HEADWORDS

... past perfect continuous – passive (simple forms) –
would conditional clauses – indirect questions –
relatives with *where/when* – gerunds after prepositions/phrases ...

I was glad. Now Hyde could not show his face to the world
again. If he did, every honest man in London would be proud
to report him to the police. *Dr Jekyll and Mr Hyde*

STAGE 5 • 1800 HEADWORDS

... future continuous – future perfect –
passive (modals, continuous forms) –
would have conditional clauses – modals + perfect infinitive ...

If he had spoken Estella's name, I would have hit him. I was so
angry with him, and so depressed about my future, that I could
not eat the breakfast. Instead I went straight to the old house.
Great Expectations

STAGE 6 • 2500 HEADWORDS

... passive (infinitives, gerunds) – advanced modal meanings –
clauses of concession, condition

When I stepped up to the piano, I was confident. It was as if I
knew that the prodigy side of me really did exist. And when I
started to play, I was so caught up in how lovely I looked that
I didn't worry how I would sound. *The Joy Luck Club*

BOOKWORMS · FANTASY & HORROR · STAGE 3

Tales of Mystery and Imagination

EDGAR ALLAN POE

Retold by Margaret Naudi

The human mind is a dark, bottomless pit, and sometimes it works in strange and frightening ways. That sound in the night . . . is it a door banging in the wind, or a murdered man knocking inside his coffin? The face in the mirror . . . is it yours, or the face of someone standing behind you, who is never there when you turn around?

These famous short stories by Edgar Allan Poe, that master of horror, explore the dark world of the imagination, where the dead live and speak, where fear lies in every shadow of the mind . . .

BOOKWORMS · CLASSICS · STAGE 3

A Christmas Carol

CHARLES DICKENS

Retold by Clare West

Christmas is humbug, Scrooge says – just a time when you find yourself a year older and not a penny richer. The only thing that matters to Scrooge is business, and making money.

But on Christmas Eve three spirits come to visit him. They take him travelling on the wings of the night to see the shadows of Christmas past, present, and future – and Scrooge learns a lesson that he will never forget.